# Out of Line

### Conceived by Julio Agustin Matos, Jr.
### Music and Lyrics by John Franceschina

## CONTENTS:

The Broadway Gypsy Robe   3
I'm So Happy I Could Dance   17
I Never Knew   21
Better Than   28
What It Was I Missed   42
Movin' On   48
Out of Line   62
Understudy Chorale   74

Copyright © 2007 by John Franceschina

Published by:

Bear Manor Media
PO Box 71426
Albany GA 31707

www.bearmanormedia.com

Printed in the United States of America on acid-free paper

ISBN 978-1-59393-104-9

# The Broadway Gypsy Robe

John Franceschina

Copyright 2007 by John Franceschina

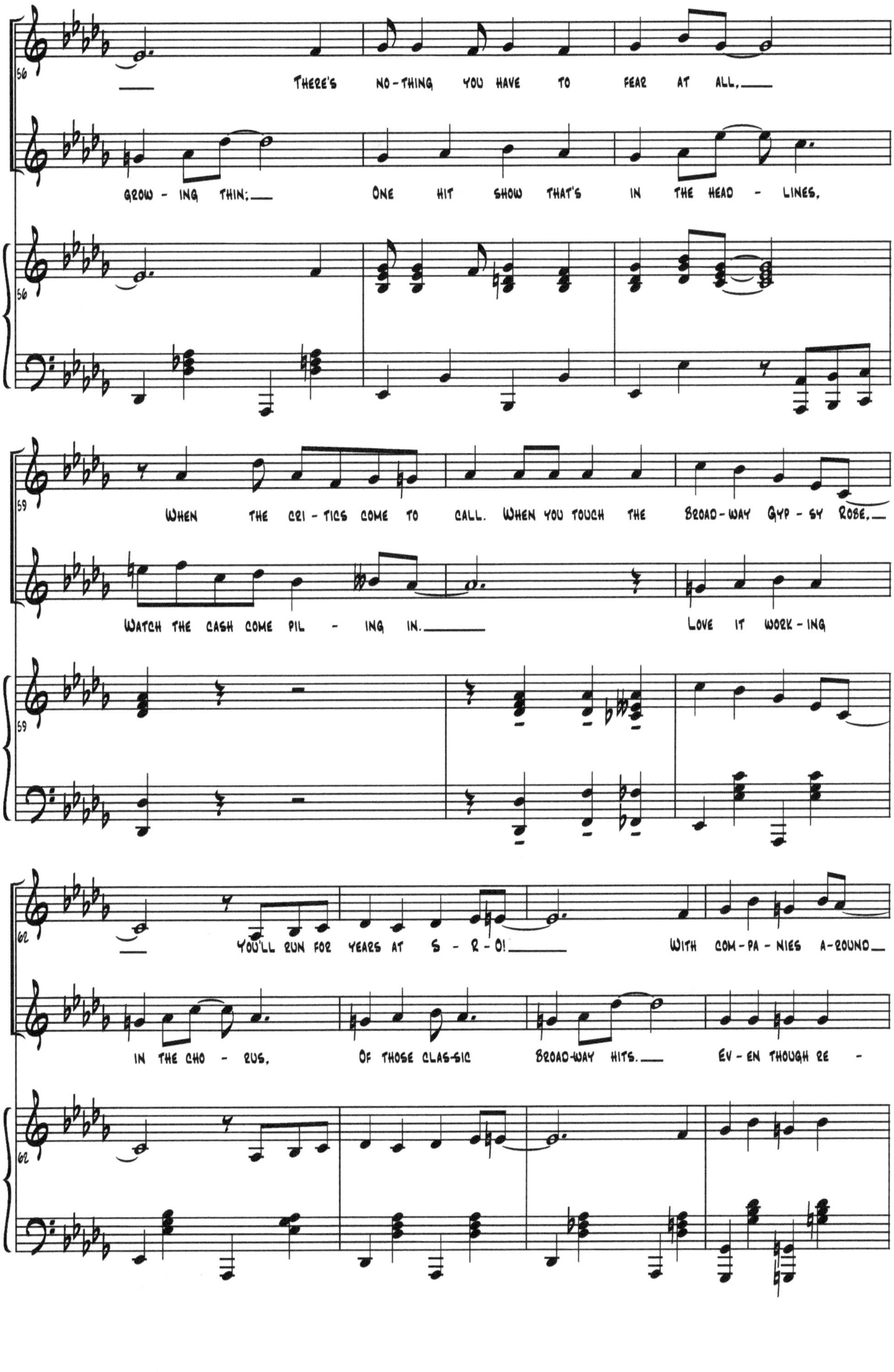
56
There's no-thing you have to fear at all.
grow - ing thin; One hit show that's in the head - lines,
59
When the cri - tics come to call. When you touch the Broad-way Gyp - sy Robe,
Watch the cash come pil - ing in. Love it work - ing
62
You'll run for years at S - R - O! With com-pa - nies a-round
in the cho - rus, Of those clas-sic Broad-way hits. Ev - en though re -

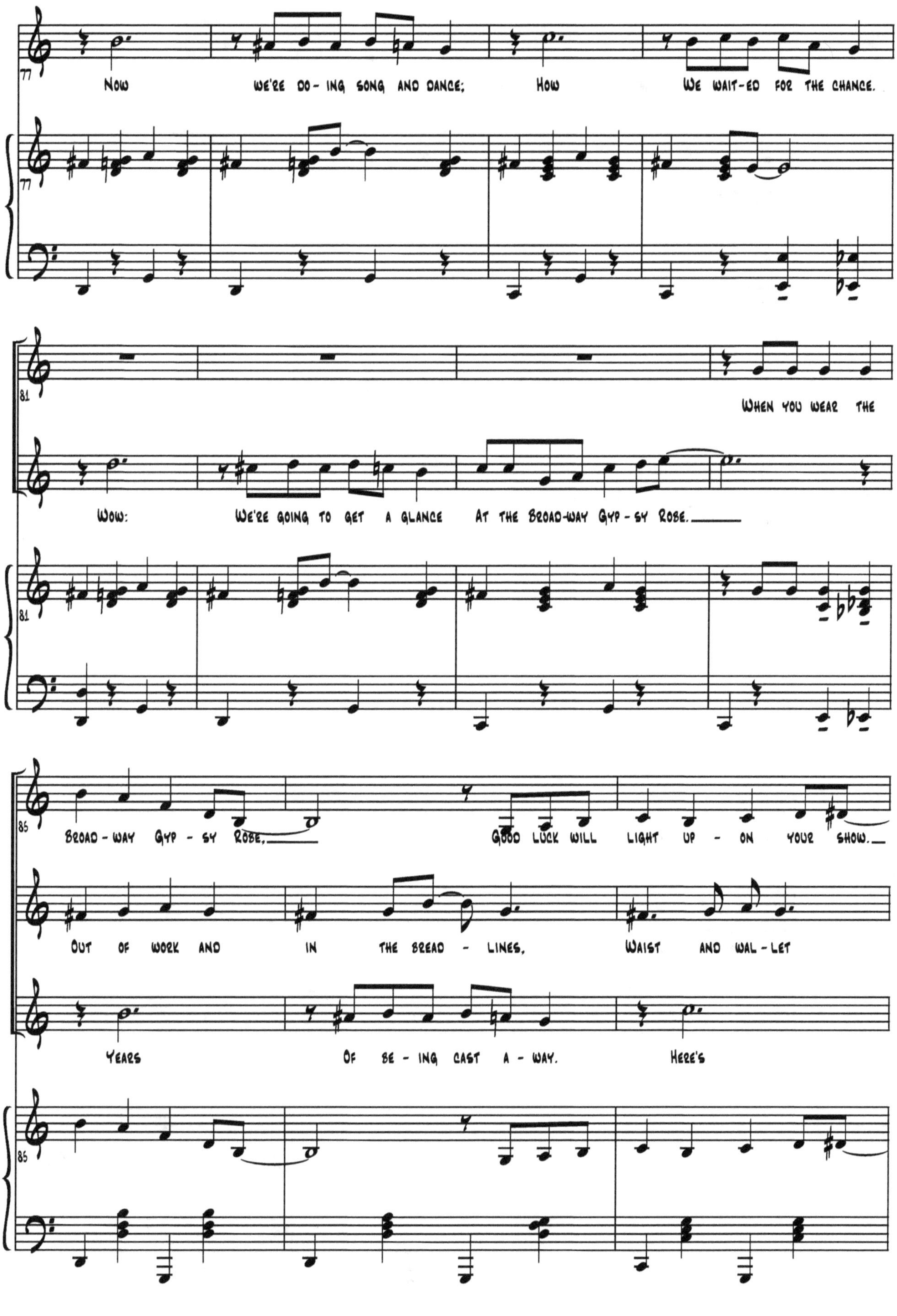
77
Now we're do - ing song and dance; How We wait - ed for the chance.
81
When you wear the
Wow: We're going to get a glance At the Broad-way Gyp - sy Robe.
85
Broad - way Gyp - sy Robe, Good luck will light up - on your show.
Out of work and in the bread - lines, Waist and wal - let
Years Of be - ing cast a - way. Here's

# I'm So Happy I Could Dance

John Franceschina

©2007 by John Franceschina

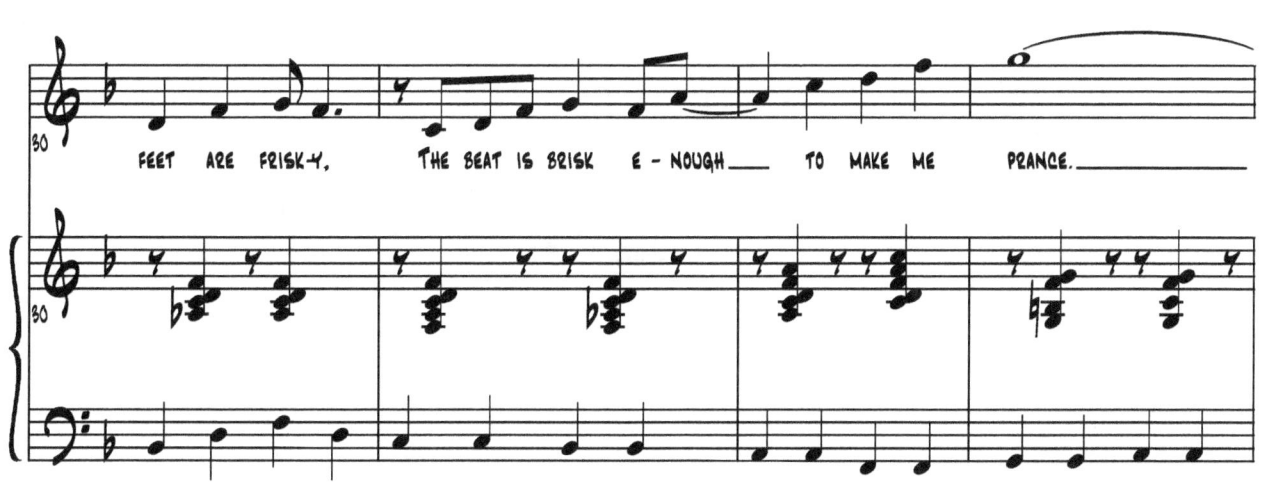

# Better Than

John Franceschina

©2006 by John Franceschina

# What It Was I Missed

John Franceschina

©2006 by John Franceschina

# Movin' On

John Franceschina

©2007 by John Franceschina

# Out of Line

John Franceschina

# Understudy Chorale

John Franceschina

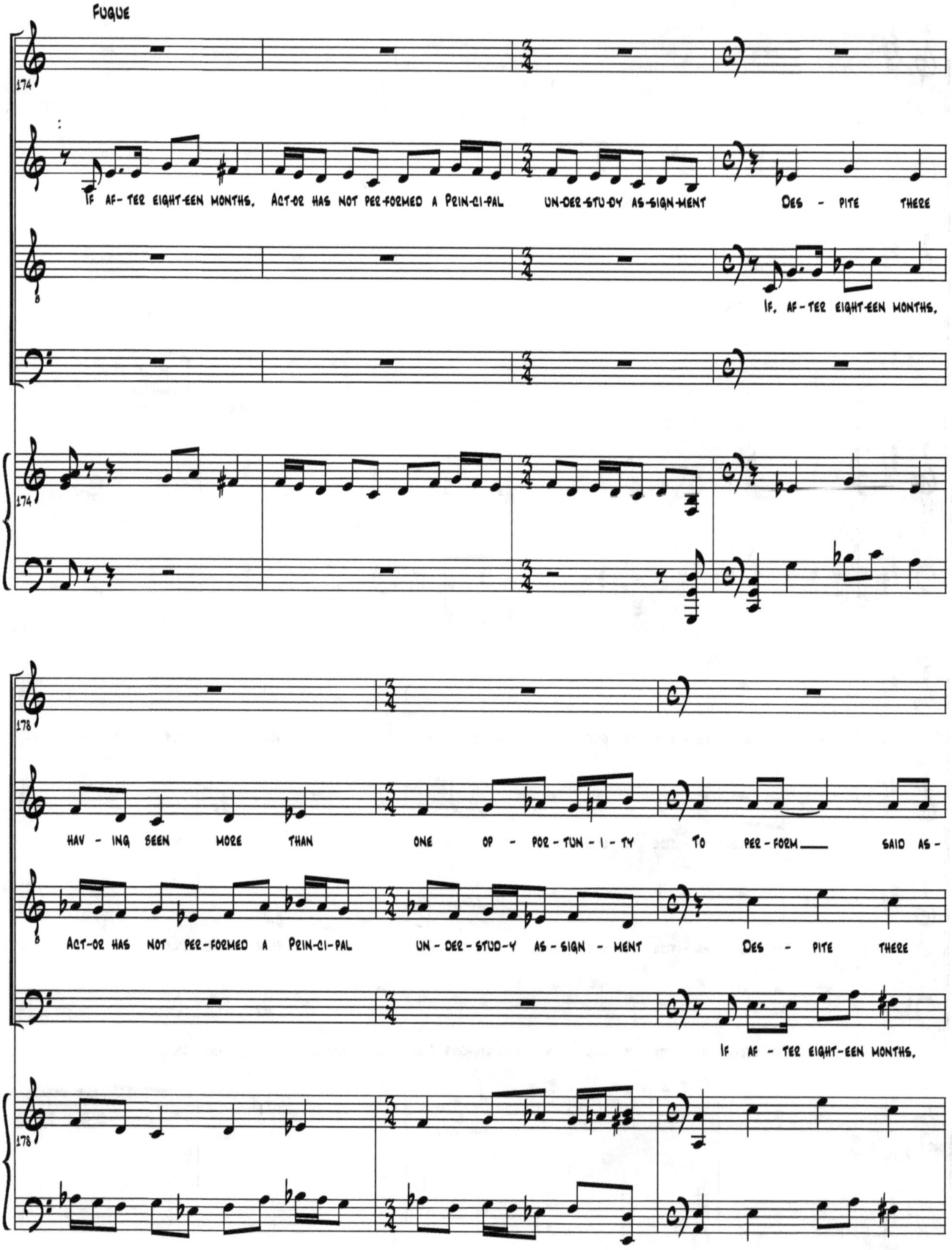
Fugue
S
A
T
B
174
If af-ter eight-een months, Act-or has not per-formed a Prin-ci-pal un-der-stu-dy as-sign-ment Des - pite there
If, af-ter eight-een months,
178
hav - ing seen more than one op - por - tun - i - ty to per - form___ said as -
Act-or has not per-formed a Prin-ci-pal un - der - stud - y as - sign - ment Des - pite there
If af - ter eight-een months,

94

www.ingramcontent.com/pod-product-compliance
Lightning Source LLC
Chambersburg PA
CBHW080407170426
43193CB00016B/2837